KT-210-469

# PRAYERS FOR PEACE

# PRAYERS

## FOR

# PEACE

Grant that before I judge my neighbor I walk in his Moccasins for many moons.

Native American proverb

# CONTENTS

This is a book about forgiveness, hope, love, understanding, and most importantly, peace and unity. Forgiveness is first, because without forgiveness there can be no hope for peace in this world.□ Peace is not solely the responsibility of our leaders. We all must do our part. We should support the peacemakers of the world as well as the political leaders who govern for honorable reasons. We should be wary of those clearly in power for their own gains. Wars should be avoided at all costs.□ In many cultures of the past, those who governed were obligated to lead their subjects into battle, should a conflict arise. But first they were obligated to seek a peaceful resolution to whatever troubles they faced. The chiefs of certain Native American tribes, for example, were chosen first and foremost for their intelligence and oratorical skills. Their bravery on the battlefield was the last qualifier. It was always preferable for the tribes for their leaders to work out their differences with dignity, and to reach an agreeable solution for both sides. If war became inevitable, however, the chief then had no alternative but to lead the tribe into battle. Sadly, this is no longer a practice. I believe there would be far fewer wars if the leaders of today's world were obligated to risk their own lives on the front lines, should they prove unable to solve their differences in a civilized manner. □ For centuries, the human race has been burdened by national and religious separations. However, extraordinary people have always managed to transcend these boundaries or "differences." Individuals such as St. Francis of Assisi, Muhatma Ghandi, The Dalai Lama, Nelson Mandela and Mother Teresa, to name just a few have exemplified themselves through their selfless contributions to the benefit of the world community. These are people who deserve our respect and support. □ Our lives are both precious and short, so we must use our resources wisely to improve our communities and help resolve social issues such as poverty, hunger, disease and injustice. I hope this book may give each and everyone of us time for reflection.

*B.Martin Pedersen, August 2002*

# ACKNOWLEDGEMENTS

This book is dedicated to the peacemakers and to the countless numbers who've sacrificed lives in the effort to bring peace to the world.

The idea for this book originated with Karen Blincoe from Denmark at an AGI (l'Alliance Graphique Internationale) Conference in Paris in October 2001—less than one month after the tragedy of September 11. I thank Karen for her concerns on the state of mankind today and the origination of this idea. My son, Bjorn Pedersen, started the editorial research. Jane Harris, Jennifer Kinon and Elizabeth Wright helped see the project to completion. My editor, Michael Porciello, stayed on top of the project from start to finish with his usual quiet and highly competent dedication. Nicole Recchia, Luis Diaz, Alexia Leitich and Joanne Sullivan in production, and especially Lauren Prigozen, the art director, were invaluable in their dedication to the typographic design quality. Thank you all.

This book would also not have been possible without the generosity of the members of the Council for a Parliament of the World's Religions and the International Interfaith Centre. Mrs. Sandy Bharat, Rev. Dirk Ficca and Lori Eisenberg, I offer my sincerest thanks. To all those who offered their contributions—Herman Agoyo, Ma Jaya Sati Bhagavati, Marcus Braybrooke, Dolly Dastoor, Dr. Homi Dhalla, Reverend Frank T. Griswold, Dadi Janki, Irfan Khan, Satish Kumar, His Holiness the Dalai Lama, Barney Leith, Rabbi Jonathan Magonet, Fr. Albert Nambiaparambil, Hema Pokharna, Dr. K.P. Seshagiri Rao, Rohinton Rivetna, Fred Rogers and Lally Warren—thank you. Due to constraints with time and space, we were unable to include all of your contributions. We hope to correct that in the future.

*B. Martin Pedersen*

The Council for a Parliament of the World's Religions (CPWR) 70 E. Lake Street, Suite 205; Chicago, IL 60601; tel: 312 629 2990; fax: 312 629 2991; www.cpwr.org
International Interfaith Centre; 2 Market Street; Oxford, OX1 3EF; United Kingdom; tel: 44(0)1865 202745; fax 44(0)1865 202746; www.interfaith-center.org

# ONE YEAR LATER: CONTINUING TO MAKE MEANING

One year later, our thoughts inevitably turn to that dazzlingly beautiful Tuesday morning of September 11, 2001, which in moments was brutally transformed by destruction and death. In a variety of ways, we are still digging our way out from under the rubble. During this year the events of that day have continued to shape our national attitudes and policies, and to leave us still dealing with questions. □ I find myself wondering how it is some could believe such terrible things were done with the presumed blessing and in the name of God. Surely such acts are not of God. And, Muslim scholars and theologians have been clear in saying that to declare so is a perversion of Islam. □ Invoking God in support of violence, murder and various patterns of oppression is nothing new, and Christianity is not immune from having been used for untoward ends. In the course of history, a common temptation has been to identify God with the interests of one's own particular group, be it a religious body, a tribe, or a nation. The uncritical assumption that my concerns and my perspectives match those of God has caused untold harm and suffering across the ages. □ I have noted with interest the recent furor caused by the challenge to the words "under God" which are part of the pledge of allegiance commonly recited in classrooms and on patriotic occasions: "...one nation, under God, indivisible with liberty and justice for all." What does it mean to be a nation under God? Does it mean our national priorities and perspectives are regarded as synonymous with God's intention and will? I think not. I believe it has a much more costly meaning: that we as a nation are called constantly to scrutinize the dynamics of our national life and relationship with other nations in the light of the deep values

we draw from Scripture…which reveal to us something of God's desires and intentions. □ If we delude ourselves that our perspectives are synonymous with God's we reduce God to a kind of totem or mascot who cheers along our actions and choices. However, if we realize that being under God means we are called to look at our lives in light of God's purposes for us, then we are opened to self-scrutiny, and indeed self-judgment and repentance. God's larger view of justness and care for the whole earth is allowed to pierce and purify our distorted and self-serving understandings of our perceived "national interests." □ If we believe—as I do—that we truly are a nation under God, then rather than covering ourselves and our actions with a self-assumed blanket of holiness, we are called to ask what the Lord requires of us. We are called to discern what it means to be faithful. □ In the days immediately following September 11, when our wounds were fresh, we had a new opportunity to ask what it means to be under God. We had a glimpse of our kinship with a larger world, where acts of terror come in many forms. By virtue of our experience, we entered into solidarity with others based on our common vulnerability. This awareness was new to us, and drew forth fear, which led us almost inevitably to thoughts of self-protection, war and retribution. Since then the world beyond us has increasingly become perceived as a hiding place for terrorists. We have thus cut ourselves off and chosen to focus almost exclusively on our "homeland." □ As a nation under God I believe we are called to claim our solidarity with our sisters and brothers around the world. We are called to ask the questions so clearly raised by the events of September 11. For example, why are we perceived with such hatred in many places around the globe? How have some of our ways of being contributed to hardship and poverty, and subsequent rage, in other parts of the world? How frequently do our international policies, economic and political, say to the world that we are not genuinely interested in anything beyond our

shores that doesn't directly benefit us? Are we unable to understand, even now, that our world is too small and too fragile for a unilateralist stance? □ In describing the church the apostle Paul uses the metaphor of a body in which the well-being of any part of the body affects the well-being of the whole. "We are members one of another," he says. Perhaps Paul's vision is one we might fruitfully apply not only to our life as a church but to our life as a nation in relationship with other nations. To live under God requires a conversion of heart and a willingness to see things not solely from the perspective of self-interest but from the perspective of God's universal care for the well-being of all people and the creation that sustains us. □ As we continue to make meaning of the events of the last year, and to live faithfully under God in these new realities, may we as the church be steadfast and strong in carrying out our mission, which is nothing less than engaging in God's project of restoring all people to unity with God and each other in Christ.

The Most Reverend Frank T. Griswold
Presiding Bishop and Primate
The Episcopal Church, USA

# MORAL GUIDES

## TEN PERFECTIONS
(Buddhism)

Generosity
Morality
Renunciation
Wisdom
Energy
Patience
Truthfulness
Resolution
Loving-Kindness
Equanimity

## TEN FETTERS OF EXISTENCE
(Buddhism)

Self-delusion
Doubt
Clinging to Ritual
Sensuous Lust
Ill Will
Greed for Fine Material Existence
Greed for Immaterial Existence
Conceit
Restlessness
Ignorance

## TEN COMMANDMENTS

(Christianity, Judiasm)

I. I am the Lord thy God, which have brought thee
out of the land of Egypt, out of the house of bondage.
Thou shalt have no other gods before me.
II. Thou shalt not take the name of the Lord thy God in vain.
III. Thou shalt not make unto thee any graven image,
or any likeness of anything that is in heaven above,
or that is in the earth beneath,
or that is in the water under the earth.
Thou shalt not bow down thyself to them, nor serve them.
IV. Remember the sabbath day, to keep it holy.
V. Honor thy father and thy mother: that thy days may be long.
VI. Thou shalt not kill.
VII. Thou shalt not commit adultery.
VIII. Thou shalt not steal.
IX. Thou shalt not bear false witness against thy neighbour.
X. Thou shalt not covet thy neighbor's house,
thou shalt not covet thy neighbor's wife,
nor his manservant, nor his maidservant, nor his ox,
nor his ass, nor anything that is thy neighbor's.

# THE TEN INDIAN COMMANDMENTS
(Native American)

Treat the Earth and all that dwell thereon with respect!
Remain close to the Great Spirit
Show great respect for your fellow beings
Work together for the benefit of all mankind!
Give assistance and kindness wherever needed
Do what you know to be right
Look after the well-being of mind and body
Dedicate a share of your efforts to the greater good
Be truthful and honest at all times
Take full responsiblity for your actions.....

# AVOIDING THE TEN EVILS
(Buddism)

The Buddha said: "All acts of living creatures become bad
by ten things, and by avoiding the ten things they become good.
There are three evils of the body, four evils of the tongue,
and three evils of the mind. The evils of the body are,
murder, theft, and adultery; of the tongue, lying,
slander, abuse, and idle talk; of the mind, covetousness, hatred,
and error. I exhort you to avoid the ten evils:

I. Kill not, but have regard for life.

II. Steal not, neither do ye rob; but help everybody
to be master of the fruits of his labor.

III. Abstain from impurity, and lead a life of chastity.

IV. Lie not, but be truthful. Speak the truth with discretion,
fearlessly and in a loving heart.

V. Invent not evil reports, neither do ye repeat them.
Carp not, but look for the good sides of your fellow-beings,
so that ye may with sincerity defend them against their enemies.

VI. Swear not, but speak decently and with dignity.

VII. Waste not the time with gossip, but speak
to the purpose or keep silence.

VIII. Covet not, nor envy, but rejoice at
the fortunes of other people.

IX. Cleanse your heart of malice and cherish no hatred,
not even against your enemies;
but embrace all living beings with kindness.

X. Free your mind of ignorance and be anxious to learn the
truth, especially in the one thing that is needful,
lest you fall a prey either to scepticism or to errors.
Scepticism will make you indifferent and errors
will lead you astray, so that you shall not
find the noble path that leads to life eternal."

# PRAYERS
# FOR
# PEACEMAKERS

## THE PEACE PRAYER OF ST. FRANCIS

Lord, make me an instrument of Thy peace;
where there is hatred, let me sow love;
where there is injury, pardon;
where there is doubt, faith;
where there is despair, hope;
where there is darkness, light;
and where there is sadness, joy.

O Divine Master,
grant that I may not so much seek
to be consoled, as to console;
to be understood, as to understand;
to be loved, as to love;
for it is in giving that we receive,
it is in pardoning that we are pardoned,
and it is in dying that we are born to eternal life.

## NATIVE AMERICAN PRAYER FOR PEACE

Oh Great Spirit of our Ancestors,
I raise my pipe to you.
To your messengers the four winds, and
to Mother Earth who provides
for your children.
Give us the wisdom to teach our children
to love, to respect, and to be kind
to each other so that they may grow
with peace of mind
Let us learn to share all good things that
you provide for us on this Earth.

Whenever I meet other people, wherever I am in different parts of the world, I am always reminded how basically similar we really are. We may wear different clothes, our skin may be of a different color, and we may speak different languages. However, these are only superficial differences. Basically, we are all the same human beings. That is what makes it possible for us to understand each other and to develop friendship and good relations. In this context let me share with you a short prayer, which is comprised of two verses by the great seventh century Indian Buddhist master, Shantideva, which gives me great inspiration in my own quest to be of benefit to others. The core of this advice is to make your life as meaningful as possible. There is nothing mysterious about it. It consists of nothing more than acting out of concern for others. And provided you undertake this practice sincerely and with persistence, you will gradually be able to reorder your habits and attitudes so that you think less about your own narrow concerns and more of others'. In doing so, you will find that you enjoy peace and happiness yourself.

The Dalai Lama

May I become at all times, both now and forever
A protector of those without protection
A guide for those who have lost their way
A ship for those with oceans to cross
A bridge for those with rivers to cross
A sanctuary for those in danger
A lamp for those without light
A place of refuge for those who lack shelter
And a servant to all in need

For as long as space endures,
And for as long as living beings remain,
Until then may I, too, abide
To dispel the misery of the world.

Shantideva

## BAHA'I PRAYER FOR PEACE

Be generous in prosperity,
and thankful in adversity.
Be fair in judgement,
and guarded in thy speech,
Be a lamp unto those who walk
in darkness, and a home
to the stranger.
Be eyes to the blind, and a guiding light
unto the feet of the erring
Be a breath of life to the body of
humankind, a dew to the soil of
the human heart,
and a fruit upon the tree of humility.

## JAINIST PRAYER FOR PEACE

Forgive do I creatures all,
and let all creatures forgive me.
Unto all have I amity, and unto none enmity.
Know that violence is the root cause of
all miseries in the world.
Violence, in fact, is the knot of bondage.
"Do not injure any living being."
This is the eternal, perrinial, and unalterable
way of spiritual life.
A weapon, howsoever powerful it may be,
can always be superseded by a superior one;
but no weapon can, however,
be superior to non-violence and love.

## SIKH PRAYER FOR PEACE

God adjudges us according to our deeds,
not the coat that we wear:
that Truth is above everything,
but higher still is truthful living.
Know that we attaineth God when we loveth,
and only victory endures in consequences
of which no one is defeated.

## CHRISTIAN PRAYER FOR PEACE

Blessed are the peacemakers,
for they shall be known as
the Children of God.
But I say to you that hear,
love your enemies,
do good to those who hate you,
bless those who curse you
pray for those who abuse you.
To those that strike you on the cheek,
offer the other one also
and from those who take away your cloak,
do not withhold your coat as well.
Give to everyone who begs from you,
and of those who take away your goods,
do not ask for them again.
And as you wish that others would do to you,
do so to them.

"In the final analysis, love is not this sentimental something that we talk about. It's not merely an emotional something. Love is creative, understanding goodwill for all men. It is the refusal to defeat any individual. When you rise to the level of love, of its great beauty and power, you seek only to defeat evil systems. Individuals who happen to be caught up in that system, you love, but you seek to defeat the system."

Martin Luther King, Jr.

"The nonviolent approach does not immediately change the heart of the oppressor. It first does something to the hearts and souls of those committed to it. It gives them new self-respect; it calls up resources of strength and courage that they didn't know they had. Finally, it reaches the opponent and so stirs his conscience that reconciliation becomes a reality. □ The ultimate weakness of violence is that it is a descending spiral, begetting the very thing it seeks to destroy. Instead of diminishing evil, it multiplies it. Through violence you murder the hater, but you do not murder hate. Returning violence for violence multiplies violence, adding deeper darkness to a night already devoid of stars. Darkness cannot drive out darkness. Only light can do that. □ We must meet hate with creative love. Love is the most durable power in the world. Love is the only force capable of transforming an enemy into a friend. □ The church must be reminded that it is not the master or the servant of the state, but rather the conscience of the state. It must be the guide and the critic of the state, and never its tool. If the church does not recapture its prophetic zeal, it will become an irrelevant social club without moral or spiritual authority. □ Power at its best is love implementing the demands of justice. Justice at its best is love correcting everything that stands against love."

Martin Luther King, Jr.

O believers, be steadfast witnesses for God with justice.
Do not let the hatred of the people make you act unjustly.
Be just, for justice is next to piety.

The Qur'an, verse 5:8

# THE PEACEMAKER

It is reported that two kingdoms were on the verge of war for the possession of a certain embankment which was disputed by them. And the Buddha, seeing the kings and their armies ready to fight, requested them to tell him the cause of their quarrels. Having heard the complaints on both sides, he said: "I understand that the embankment has value for some of your people; has it any intrinsic value aside from its service to your men?"

"It has no intrinsic value whatever," was the reply.

The Tathagata continued: "Now when you go to battle is it not sure that many of your men will be slain and that you yourselves, O kings, are liable to lose your lives?"

And they said: "It is sure that many will be slain and our own lives be jeopardized."

"The blood of men, however," said Buddha, "has it less intrinsic value than a mound of earth?"

"No," the kings said, "The lives of men and above all the lives of kings, are priceless."

Then the Tathagata concluded: "Are you going to stake that which is priceless against that which has no intrinsic value whatever?" The wrath of the two monarchs abated, and they came to a peaceable agreement.

The Gospel of Buddha, Chapter 77
compiled by Paul Carus, 1894

Nor an eye for an eye and a tooth for a tooth, for him who counts no man his enemy, but all his neighbors, and therefore can never stretch out his hand for vengeance.

St. Irenaeus

But I say to you that hear, "Love your enemies, do good to those who hate you, bless those who curse you, pray for those who abuse you. To him who strikes you on the cheek, offer the other also; and from him who takes away your coat do not withhold even your shirt. Give to every one who begs from you; and of him who takes away your goods do not ask them again. And as you wish that men would do to you, do so to them. If you love those who love you, what credit is that to you? For even sinners love those who love them. And if you do good to those who do good to you, what credit is that to you? For even sinners do the same. And if you lend to those from whom you hope to receive, what credit is that to you? Even sinners lend to sinners, to receive as much again. But love your enemies, and do good, and lend, expecting nothing in return; and your reward will be great, and you will be sons of the Most High; for he is kind to the ungrateful and the selfish. Be merciful, even as your Father is merciful. Judge not, and you will not be judged; condemn not, and you will not be condemned; forgive, and you will be forgiven; give, and it will be given to you; good measure, pressed down, shaken together, running over, will be put into your lap. For the measure you give will be the measure you get back."

Luke 6:27-38

Who among you is wise and understanding? Let him show by his good behavior his deeds in the gentleness of wisdom. But if you have bitter jealousy and selfish ambition in your heart, do not be arrogant and so lie against the truth. This wisdom is not that which comes down from above, but is earthly, natural, demonic. For where jealousy and selfish ambition exist, there is disorder and every evil thing. But the wisdom from above is first pure, then peaceable, gentle, reasonable, full of mercy and good fruits, unwavering, without hypocrisy. And the seed whose fruit is righteousness is sown in peace by those who make peace.

James 3:13-18

But I tell you, Do not resist an evil person. If someone strikes you on the right cheek, turn to him the other also.

Matthew 5:39

Do not take revenge, my friends, but leave room for God's wrath, for it is written: "'It is mine to avenge; I will repay,' says the Lord." On the contrary: "If your enemy is hungry, feed him; if he is thirsty, give him something to drink. In doing this, you will heap burning coals on his head." Do not be overcome by evil, but overcome evil with good.

Romans 12:19-21

Do not repay evil with evil or insult with insult,
but with blessing, because to this you were called
so that you may inherit a blessing.

1 Peter 3:9

There is only one Lawgiver and Judge,
the one who is able to save and destroy.
But you—who are you to judge your neighbor?

James 4:12

## HINDU PEACE PRAYER

I desire neither earthly kingdom,
nor even freedom from birth and death.
I desire only the deliverance
from grief of all those afflicted by misery.
Oh Lord, lead us from the unreal to the real;
from darkness to light,
from death to immortality.
May there be peace in celestial regions.
May there be peace on earth.
May the waters be appeasing.
May herbs be wholesome
and may trees and plants bring peace to all.
May all beneficent beings bring peace to us.
May thy wisdom spread peace all through the world.
May all things be a source of peace to all and to me.

Grant us peace. Your most precious gift, O Eternal Source of Peace, and give us the will to proclaim its message to all the peoples of the earth. Bless our country, that it may always be a stronghold of peace, and its advocate among the nations. May contentment reign within its borders, health and happiness within its homes. Strengthen the bonds of friendship among the inhabitants of all lands. And may the love of Your name hallow every home and every heart. Blessed is the Eternal God, the source of Peace.

From Gates of Prayer: The New Union Prayer Book,
by the Central Conferences of American Rabbis

## RASTAFARIAN PEACE PRAYER

O thou God of Ethiopia,
thou God of divine majesty,
thy spirit come within our hearts
to dwell in the parts of righteousness.
That the hungry be fed, the sick nourished,
the aged protected and the infant cared for.

Goodness is stronger than evil;
Love is stronger than hate;
Light is stronger than darkness;
Victory is ours through him who loves us.

Archbishop Desmond Tutu

# PRAYERS
# FOR
# INNER PEACE

## PRAYER FOR PEACE
## ADAPTED FROM THE UPANISHADS

Lead me from death to life,
from falsehood to truth.
Lead me from despair to hope,
from fear to trust.
Lead me from hate to love,
from war to peace.
Let peace fill our heart, our world, our universe.

(Suggested by Satish Kumar)

O God, make us children of quietness,
and heirs of peace.

St. Clement of Rome

May I be filled with loving kindness.
May I be well.
May I be peaceful and at ease.
May I be happy.

Ancient Tibetan Buddhist Meditation

## ZOROASTRIAN PRAYER

In this house
May thy acceptance smite defiance
Peace triumph over discord
Generosity over greed
Devotion over arrogance
Honest discussion dominate over falsehood
May righteousness prevail
Over evil of lies

Yasna 60.5

Oh, Great Spirit,
whose voice I hear in the winds
and whose breath gives life to all the world, hear me.
I am small and weak.
I need your strength and wisdom.

Let me walk in beauty and make my eyes
ever behold the red and purple sunset.
Make my hands respect the things you have made
and my ears sharp to hear your voice.
Make me wise so that I may understand
the things you have taught my people.
Let me learn the lessons you have hidden
in every leaf and rock.

I seek strength, not to be superior to my brother,
but to fight my greatest enemy—myself.
Make me always ready to come to you
with clean hands and straight eyes,
so when life fades, as the fading sunset,
my spirit will come to you
without shame.

Chief Yellow Lark (Lakota American Indian)

In thee, O Lord, do I take refuge...rescue me.
Be thou to me a rock of refuge;
Forsake me not when my strength is spent.

Psalm 71:1-3

## HINDU PRAYER FOR PEACE

Oh God, lead us from the unreal to the real.
Oh God, lead us from darkness to light.
Oh God, lead us from death to immortality.
Shanti, Shanti, Shanti unto all.

Oh Lord God almighty,
may there be peace in celestial regions.
May there be peace on Earth.
May the waters be appeasing.
May herbs be wholesome,
and may trees and plants bring peace to all.

May all beneficent beings bring peace to us.
May thy Vedic Law propogate peace all through the world.
May all things be a source of peace to us.
And may thy peace itself, bestow peace on all
and may that peace come to me also.

Deep peace of the running wave to you.
Deep peace of the flowing air to you.
Deep peace of the quiet earth to you.
Deep peace of the shining stars to you.
Deep peace of the infinite peace to you.

Adapted from ancient Gaelic Runes

If there is to be peace in the world,
There must be peace in the nations.

If there is to be peace in the nations,
There must be peace in the cities.

If there is to be peace in the cities,
There must be peace between neighbors.

If there is to be peace between neighbors,
There must be peace in the home.

If there is to be peace in the home,
There must be peace in the heart.

Lao-Tse, Chinese Philospher (6th Century BCE)

Live your life that the fear of death
can never enter your heart.
Trouble no one about his religion.
Respect others in their view,
and demand that they respect yours.
Love your life, perfect your life,
Beautify all things in your life.
Seek to make your life long
and of service to your people.

Prepare a noble death song for the day
when you go over the great divide.
Always give a word or a sign of salute when meeting
or passing a friend, or even a stranger, when in a lonely place.
Show respect to all people but grovel to none.
When you arise in the morning, give thanks for the light
and for your life, for your strength.
Give thanks for your food and for the joy of living.
If you see no reason for giving thanks,
the fault lies only in yourself.
Touch not the poisonous firewater.
Abuse no one and nothing,
For abuse turns the wise ones to fools
and robs the spirit of its vision.

When it comes your time to die, be not like those
whose hearts are filled with fear of death,
so that when their time comes they weep and pray
for a little more time to live their lives over again
In a different way.
"Sing your death song and die like a hero going home."

Tecumseh

## SAMSARA AND NIRVANA

Look about and contemplate life! Everything is transient and nothing endures. There is birth and death, growth and decay; there is combination and separation. The glory of the world is like a flower: it stands in full bloom in the morning and fades in the heat of the day. □ Wherever you look, there is a rushing and a struggling, and an eager pursuit of pleasure. There is a panic flight from pain and death, and hot are the flames of burning desires. The world is Vanity Fair, full of changes and transformations. All is Samsara, the turning Wheel of Existence. □ Is there nothing permanent in the world? Is there in the universal turmoil no resting-place where our troubled heart can find peace? Is there nothing everlasting? Oh, that we could have cessation of anxiety, that our burning desires would be extinguished! When shall the mind become tranquil and composed? □ The Buddha, our Lord, was grieved at the ills of life. He saw the vanity of worldly happiness and sought salvation in the one thing that will not fade or perish, but will abide for ever and ever. □ You who long for life, learn that immortality is hidden in transiency. You who wish for happiness without the sting of regret, lead a life of righteousness. You who yearn for riches, receive treasures that are eternal. Truth is wealth, and a life of truth is happiness.

The Gospel of Buddha, Chapter 2
compiled by Paul Carus, 1894

Blessed is the man who finds wisdom, the man who gains understanding, for she is more profitable than silver and yields better returns than gold. She is more precious than rubies; nothing you desire can compare with her. Long life is in her right hand; in her left hand are riches and honor. Her ways are pleasant ways, and all her paths are peace. She is a tree of life to those who embrace her; those who lay hold of her will be blessed. By wisdom the Lord laid the earth's foundations, by understanding he set the heavens in place; By his knowledge the deeps were divided, and the clouds let drop the dew.

Proverbs 3:13-20

# ZOROASTRIAN PRAYER FOR PEACE

We pray to eradicate
All the misery in the world;
That understanding triumph over ignorance,
That generosity triumph over indifference,
That trust triumph over contempt,
And that truth triumph over falsehood.

I solemnly dedicate myself to the truth,
And to the true spoken word,
To true action.

I dedicate myself to reason which causes peace,
And teaches self-sacrifice.

Through the cooperation of all the peoples of the world,
May we all be one in justice,
And may we all benefit from each other
And help all those that are need.

Through words and deeds, make in me
A peaceful attitude toward all,
Seeking to renew my life
And make it as you wish it,
A life of truth.

(Suggested by Rohinton Rivetna)

## SAMSARA AND NIRVANA

Learn to distinguish between Self and Truth. Self is the cause of selfishness and the source of evil; truth cleaves to no self; it is universal and leads to justice and righteousness. Self, that which seems to those who love their self as their being, is not the eternal, the everlasting, the imperishable. Seek not self, but seek the truth. □ If we liberate our souls from our petty selves, wish no ill to others, and become clear as a crystal diamond reflecting the light of truth, what a radiant picture will appear in us mirroring things as they are, without the admixture of burning desires, without the distortion of erroneous illusion, without the agitation of clinging and unrest.

The Gospel of Buddha, Chapter 2
compiled by Paul Carus, 1894

I forgive all beings,
I ask forgiveness from all beings,
I make friends with all beings,
I have no enemies.

From the Jain text, Pratikraman Sutra
(Suggested by Satish Kumar)

Meri Bhavana has always been one of my favorite Jain prayers. I like this prayer very much as I have recited it since childhood and it has always helped me make choices that have enriched my life and enhanced others life too. This has also helped me understand the interconnectedness of life and reach an understanding of how I can make life wonderful.

Hema Pokharna

## MERI BHAVANA

May I be friendly towards all beings,
May I delight in the qualities of the virtuous ones,
May I practice utmost compassion for afflicted beings,
May I be equanimous towards those who are not well
disposed towards me,
May my soul have such dispositions as these for ever.

"A human being is part of the whole called by us universe, a part limited in time and space. We experience ourselves, our thoughts and feelings as something separate from the rest. A kind of optical delusion of consciousness. This delusion is a kind of prison for us, restricting us to our personal desires and to affection for a few persons nearest to us. Our task must be to free ourselves from the prison by widening our circle of compassion to embrace all living creatures and the whole of nature in its beauty. We shall require a substantially new manner of thinking if mankind is to survive."

Albert Einstein

Do not feed your spirit on anything apart from God.
Cast away all cares and let peace and reconciliation
fill your heart.

St. John of the Cross

Create in me a pure heart, O God,
and renew a steadfast spirit within me.
Do not cast me from your presence
or take your Holy Spirit from me.
Restore to me the joy of salvation
and grant me a willing spirit, to sustain me.

Psalm 51:10-12 (King David)

## ANCIENT VEDIC PRAYER

From untruth lead us to Truth.
From darkness lead us to Light.
From death lead us to Immortality.
Om Peace, Peace, Peace.

## THE SERENITY PRAYER

God, grant me the serenity
to accept the things I cannot change;
the courage to change the things I can;
and the wisdom to know the difference.

Reinhold Niebuhr

# EULOGY FOR THE MARTYRED CHILDREN

Now I say to you in conclusion, life is hard, at times as hard as crucible steel. It has its bleak and difficult moments. Like the ever-flowing waters of the river, life has its moments of drought and its moments of flood. Like the ever-changing cycle of the seasons, life has the soothing warmth of its summers and the piercing chill of its winters. But if one will hold on, he will discover that God walks with him, and that God is able to lift you from the fatigue of despair to the buoyancy of hope and transform dark and desolate valleys into sunlit paths of inner peace.

Martin Luther King, Jr.

Oh Allah!
I consult You as You are all Knowing,
and I seek ability from Your power
and I ask you for Your great favor,
for You have power, but I do not,
and You have knowledge, but I do not,
and You know all hidden matters.

Oh Allah!
If You know that this matter is good for me in my religion,
my livelihood and my life in the Hereafter,
then make it easy and bless it;
and if You know that this matter is evil for me in my religion,
my livelihood and my life in the Hereafter,
then keep it away from me and keep me away from it,
and choose what is good for me wherever it is,
and make me pleased with it.

Prophet Muhammad

Hold to forgiveness and enjoin good;
turn aside from the foolish.

The Qur'an, verse 7:199

"I expect to pass through life but once. If, therefore, there be any kindness I can show, or any good thing I can do for any fellow being, let me do it now...as I shall not pass this way again."

William Penn

"The purpose of life is not to be happy. It is to useful, to be honorable, to be compassionate, to have it make some difference that you have lived, and live well."

Ralph Waldo Emerson

## GAIAN PRAYER

Peace.
Peace She says to me.
Peace to your soul.
I am the beauty in the leaf.
I am the echo in a baby's laugh.
I am your Mother.
I am the joy in the heart that beats.
I am the free woman.
I am the one who breaks the shackles of oppression.
You are my hands and feet.

Jason Clark

## PRAYER AT TIME OF ADVERSITY

I think over again my small adventures
My fears,
Those small ones that seemed so big,
For all the vital things
I had to get and reach.
And yet there is only one great thing,
The only thing,
To live to see the great day that dawns
And the light that fills the world.

Inuit Indian Prayer

PRAYERS
FOR
PEACE
FOR ALL
OF
HUMANITY

Violence never again!
War never again!
Terrorism never again!
In God's name,
may all religions bring upon earth
justice and peace,
forgiveness, life and love!

Pope John Paul II

O God, we pray for all those in our world
who are suffering from injustice:
For those who are discriminated against
because of their race, color or religion;
For those imprisoned
for working for the relief of oppression;
For those who are hounded
for speaking the inconvenient truth;
For those tempted to violence
as a cry against overwhelming hardship;
For those deprived of reasonable health and education;
For those suffering from hunger and famine;
For those too weak to help themselves
and who have no one else to help them;
For the unemployed who cry out
for work but do not find it.
We pray for anyone of our acquaintance
who is personally affected by injustice.
Forgive us, Lord, if we unwittingly share in the conditions
or in a system that perpetuates injustice.
Show us how we can serve your children
and make your love practical by washing their feet.

Mother Teresa

## TRADITIONAL BUDDHIST PRAYER

May all beings have happiness and the causes of happiness;
May all be free from sorrow and the causes of sorrow;
May all never be separated from the sacred happiness
which is sorrowless;
And may all live in equanimity,
without too much attachment
and too much aversion,
And live believing in the equality of all that lives.

Make us worthy, Lord, to serve our fellow men
throughout the world
who live and die in poverty and hunger.
Give them through our hands this day their daily bread,
and by our understanding love, give peace and joy.

Mother Teresa

## SHINTO PRAYER FOR PEACE

Although the people living across the ocean
surrounding us, I believe are all our brothers and sisters,
why are there constant troubles in this world?
Why do winds and waves rise in the oceans surrounding us?
I only earnestly wish that the wind will
soon puff away all the clouds which are
hanging over the tops of mountains.

Let us be united;
Let us speak in harmony;
Let our minds apprehend alike.
Common be our prayer,
Common be the end of our assembly;
Common be our resolution;
Common be our deliberations.
Alike be our feelings;
Unified be our hearts;
Common be our intentions;
Perfect be our unity.

From the Rig Veda

## PRAYER FOR PEACE IN THE MIDDLE EAST

O God, as Muslims, Jews and Christians,
We acknowledge that thou
Hast made of one blood
All the nations of the earth.
Thou dost love all of us
As if all were but one,
And dost care for each
As if thou hadst naught else
To care for.
Remembering such love,
May we not weary in our efforts
To fashion out of our failures today
some great good
for all thy people tomorrow.
And not unto us O God,
not unto us,
but unto Thy name
be the glory.

Prepared by a Christian, a Jew and a Muslim, from "Pressing for Peace"

Have you heard the story that came out of the Seattle Special Olympics? □ For the 100-yard-dash there were nine contestants, all of them so-called physically or mentally disabled. All nine of them assembled at the starting line and at the sound of the gun, they took off. But one little boy didn't get very far. He stumbled and fell and hurt his knee and began to cry. □ The other eight children heard the boy crying. They slowed down, turned around and ran back to him—every one of them ran back to him. One little girl with Down syndrome bent down and kissed the boy and said, "This will make it better." The little boy got up, and he and the rest of the runners linked arms together and joyfully walked to the finish line. □ They all finished the race at the same time. And when they did, everyone in the stadium stood up and clapped and whistled and cheered for a long, long time. People who were there are still telling the story with obvious delight. And you know why? □ Because deep down we know that what matters in this life is more than winning for ourselves. What really matters is helping others win, too, even if it means slowing down and changing our course now and then.

As retold by Fred Rogers at the 2002 commencement
of Chatham College, Pittsburgh (Author Unknown)

If one member suffers, all suffer together.

1 Corinthians 12:26

Move beyond any attachment to names. Every war and every conflict between human beings has happened because of some disagreement about names. It's such an unnecessary foolishness, because just beyond the arguing there's a long table of companionship, set and waiting for us to sit down. □ What is praised is one, so the praise is one too, many jugs being poured into a huge basin. All religions, all this singing, one song. The differences are just illusion and vanity. Sunlight looks slightly different on this wall than it does on that wall and a lot different on this other one, but it is still one light. We have borrowed these clothes, these time-and-space personalities, from a light, and when we praise, we pour them back in.

Mevlana Jelaluddin Rumi (13th Century) translation by Coleman Barks

Here there is no Greek or Jew, circumcised or uncircumcised, barbarian, Scythian, slave or free, but Christ is all, and is in all.

Colossians 3:11

## PRAYER FOR INTERFAITH MEETINGS

God of all creation, we stand in awe before You, impelled by visions of human harmony. We are children of many traditions—inheritors of shared wisdom and tragic misunderstandings, of proud hopes and humble successes. Now it is time for us to meet—in memory and truth, in courage and trust, in love and promise. □ In that which we share, let us see the common prayer of humanity; in that in which we differ, let us wonder at human freedom; in our unity and our differences, let us know the uniqueness that is God. □ May our courage match our convictions, and our integrity match our hope. May our faith in You bring us closer to each other. May our meeting with past and present bring blessing for the future.

From Forms of Prayer for Jewish Worship Vol I Daily,
Sabbath and Occasional Prayers Edited by the Assembly of Rabbis of the Reform
Synagogues of Great Britain, (1977) (Suggested by Rabbi Jonathan Magonet)

# PRAYER FOR INTERNATIONAL UNDERSTANDING

God of peace, be with those who guide the destinies of the world so that an end may come to boasting and vainglory, and the reign of arrogance dwindle in our time. Give them the courage to speak the truth and the humility to listen. Help us all to put the good of others above our own ambitions, and the truth which does not profit us above the lie which does. So may we stand upright, freed from the burden of fear and the weight of suspicion, learning to trust each other. □ Help each one of us to bring our own offering of understanding, and our own sacrifice for peace, so that we are at peace with ourselves and live in peace with those around us. Then in tranquility may we all go forward to build Your kingdom in the world until the earth shall be filled with Your knowledge as the waters cover the sea.

From Forms of Prayer for Jewish Worship Vol I Daily, Sabbath and Occasional Prayers Edited by the Assembly of Rabbis of the Reform Synagogues of Great Britain, (1977) (Suggested by Rabbi Jonathan Magonet)

Almighty God, kindle, we pray, in every heart the true love of peace, and guide with your wisdom those who take counsel for the nations of the earth, that in tranquility your dominion may increase until the earth is filled with the knowledge of your love.

Book of Common Prayer

Hearken with your ears to these best counsels,
Reflect upon them with illumined judgment.
Let each one choose his creed with that freedom of choice
each must have at great events.
O ye, be awake to these, my announcements.

Gathas of Zarathushtra (Yasna 30:2)

Pray not for Arab or Jew,
for Palestinian or Israeli,
but pray rather for yourselves
that you may not divide them in your prayers,
but keep them both together in your hearts.

Rabbi Stanley A. Ringler

## PRAYER FOR THE PEACE OF JERUSALEM

Gracious God, you have promised through your prophets
that Jerusalem will be home to many peoples,
mothers to many nations.

Hear our prayers that Jerusalem, the city of your visitation,
may be for all—Jews, Christians and Muslims—
a place to dwell with you
and to encounter one another in peace.

Churches for Middle East Peace

This prayer was written by Bishop George Appleton, a personal friend and mentor, who was a former Anglican Archbishop in Jerusalem, a Chairman of the World Congress of Faiths and Editor of the Oxford Book of Prayer. I like this prayer as it is one which people of most religions can say together. It links the need for inner peace and peace in the world.

Reverend Marcus Braybrooke,
President of the World Congress of Faiths

O God of many names,
Lover of all people,
Give peace in our hearts,
in our homes,
in our world,
in our universe:
The peace of our need
The peace of your will.
Amen.

Bishop George Appleton

Increasingly we value diversity. And the diversity of humankind is a great richness, like the many different kinds, colors, shapes and sizes of the flowers in a wondrous garden. But we must remember that there is just the one human garden and that we are all the flowers of that garden. Unity expresses itself in diversity. Without diversity, unity brings only dull uniformity. But without unity, diversity results only in division. So now it is important to consider the world with the eye of oneness. As 'Abdu'l-Bahá, the eldest son of the Founder of the Bahá'í Faith, Bahá'u'lláh writes:

Barney Leith, Secretary General, Bahá'í Community of the UK

O peoples of the world! The Sun of Truth hath risen to illumine the whole earth, and to spiritualize the community of man. Laudable are the results and the fruits thereof, abundant the holy evidences deriving from this grace. This is mercy unalloyed and purest bounty; it is light for the world and all its peoples; it is harmony and fellowship, and love and solidarity; indeed it is compassion and unity, and the end of foreignness; it is the being at one, in complete dignity and freedom, with all on earth. □ The Blessed Beauty saith: "Ye are all the fruits of one tree, the leaves of one branch." Thus hath He likened this world of being to a single tree, and all its peoples to the leaves thereof, and the blossoms and fruits. It is needful for the bough to blossom, and leaf and fruit to flourish, and upon the interconnection of all parts of the world-tree, dependeth the flourishing of leaf and blossom, and the sweetness of the fruit. □ For this reason must all human beings powerfully sustain one another and seek for everlasting life; and for this reason must the lovers of God in this contingent world become the mercies and the blessings sent forth by that clement King of the seen and unseen realms. Let them purify their sight and behold all humankind as leaves and blossoms and fruits of the tree of being. Let them at all times concern themselves with doing a kindly thing for one of their fellows, offering to someone love, consideration, thoughtful help. Let them see no one as their enemy, or as wishing them ill, but think of all humankind as their friends; regarding the alien as an intimate, the stranger as a companion, staying free of prejudice, drawing no lines.

'Abdu'l-Bahá

## BUDDHIST PRAYER FOR PEACE

May all beings everywhere
plagued with sufferings of body and mind
quickly be freed from their illnesses.

May those frightened cease to be afraid
and may those bound be free.

May the powerless find power,
and may people think of befriending one another.

May those who find themselves
in trackless, fearful wildernesses—
the children, the aged, the unprotected—
be guarded by beneficent celestials,
and may they quickly attain Buddhahood.

Eternal God, in whose perfect kingdom no sword is drawn but the sword of righteousness, no strength is known but the strength of love: So mightily spread abroad your Spirit, that all peoples may be gathered under the banner of the Prince of Peace, as children of one Father; to whom be dominion and glory, now and for ever. Amen.

Book of Common Prayer

May the whole world enjoy
good health,
long life,
prosperity,
happiness
and peace.

Vethathiri Maharishi (Kundalini Yoga Master)

## HINDU PRAYER FOR PEACE

Cultivate friendship which will conquer all hearts.
Look upon others as thyself.
Renounce war;
Forswear competition.
Give up aggression on others, as this is wrong.
Wide mother earth, our mother, is here
ready to give us all desires.
We have the Lord, our Father, compassionate to all.
Ye people of the world!
Restrain yourselves.
Give, be kind.
May all people be happy and prosperous.

Jagatguru Shri Sankaracharya

Oh Almighty! May he protect all of us!
May he cause us to enjoy!
May we acquire strength together.
May our knowledge become brilliant!
May we not hate each other!
Oh Almighty! May there be peace everywhere!

Oh Almighty! May everybody be happy!
May all be free from ailments!
May we see that all is auspicious!
May no one be subject to miseries!
Oh Almighty! May there be peace everywhere!

From the Kathopanisada

## SUFI PRAYER FOR PEACE

Send Thy peace O Lord, which is
perfect and everlasting,
that our souls may radiate peace.

Send Thy peace O Lord, that we
may think, act and speak harmoniously.

Send Thy peace O Lord, that we
may be contented and thankful for
Thy bountiful gifts.

Send Thy peace O Lord, that amidst
our worldly strife, we may enjoy Thy bliss.

Send Thy peace O Lord, that we
may endure all, tolerate all, in the thought of
Thy grace and mercy.

Send Thy peace O Lord, that our lives
may become a Divine vision and in Thy light,
all darkness may vanish.

Send Thy peace O Lord, our Father and Mother,
that we Thy children on Earth may all
unite in one family.

Pir-o-Murshid Inayat Khan

## NATIVE AMERICAN PRAYER FOR THE WHITE MAN

And now, Grandfather,
I ask you to bless the white man.
He needs your wisdom, your guidance.
You see, for so long he has tried to destroy my people,
and only feels comfortable when given power.
Bless them, show them the peace we understand;
teach them humility.
For I fear they will someday destroy themselves
and their children
as they have done to Mother Earth.
I plead, I cry, after all, they are my brothers…

PRAYERS
FOR
PEACE
DURING
WARTIME

## NAVAL SERVICEMAN'S PRAYER (WORLD WAR II)

All mighty Father,
whose way is in the sea
and whose paths are in the great waters
whose command is over all and whose love never faileth:
Let me be aware of Thy presence
and obedient to Thy will.
Keep me true to my best self,
guarding me against dishonesty in purpose and in deed,
and helping me so to live
that I can stand unashamed and unafraid before my shipmates,
my loved ones, and Thee.

Protect those in whose love I live.
Give me the will to do the work of a man
and to accept my share of responsibilities
with a strong heart and a cheerful mind.
Make me considerate of those intrusted to my leadership
and faithful to the duties my country has intrusted to me.
Let my uniform remind me daily
of the traditions of the Service of which I am a part.

If I am inclined to doubt, steady my faith;
if I am tempted, make me strong to resist;
if I should miss the mark, give me courage to try again.
Guide me with the light of truth and
keep before me the life of Him
by whose example and help
I trust to obtain the answer to my prayer.

## THE SUBMARINER'S PRAYER

Almighty, Everlasting God,
the Protector of all those who put their trust in Thee:
hear our prayers on behalf of Thy servants
who sail their vessels beneath the seas.
We beseech Thee to keep in Thy sustaining care
all who are in submarines,
that they may be delivered
from the hidden dangers of the deep.
Grant them courage,
and a devotion to fulfill their duties,
that they may better serve Thee and their native land.
Though acquainted with the depths of the ocean,
deliver them from the depths of despair
and the dark hours of the absence of friendliness
and grant them a good ship's spirit.
Bless all their kindred and loved ones
from whom they are separated.
When they surface their ships,
may they praise Thee for Thou art there
as well as in the deep.
Fill them with Thy Spirit
that they may be sure in their reckonings,
unwavering in duty,
high in purpose,
and upholding the honor of their nation.

"It's time for the quiet voices to get loud. We soft-spoken peace lovers must raise our voices and let it be known that we can lovingly and aggressively reach across those invisible lines that divide us into competing groups. We must work hard to understand who our 'enemies' are. We have to listen hard in order to articulate, loudly and clearly, the truths we have come to understand. We can and must pursue peace with furious energy and focus."

Cantor Cathy Schwartzman,
Temple of Universal Judaism, New York City

"Peace cannot be achieved through violence; it can only be attained through understanding."

Albert Einstein

It may be that God will bring about friendship between you
and those whom you hold to be your enemies.

The Qur'an, Verse 60:7

# I WILL FIGHT NO MORE FOREVER

I will fight no more forever.
I am tired of fighting.
Our chiefs are killed.
Looking Glass is dead.
Toohulhulsote is dead.
The old men are all dead.
It is the young men who say no and yes.
He who led the young men is dead.
It is cold and we have no blankets.
The little children are freezing to death.
My people, some of them,
Have run away to the hills
And have no blankets, no food.
No one knows where they are
Perhaps they are freezing to death.
I want to have time to look for my children
And see how many of them I can find.
Maybe I shall find them among the dead.
Hear me, my chiefs, I am tired.
My heart is sad and sick.
From where the sun now stands
I will fight no more forever.

Surrender Speech by Chief Joseph of the Nez Perce, 1877

# PRAYERS
# FOR
# PEACEFUL
# TIMES

## ISLAMIC PRAYER FOR PEACE

In the name of Allah,
the beneficent, the merciful.
Praise be to the Lord of the
Universe who has created us and
made us into tribes and nations.
That we may know each other, not that
we may despise each other.
If the enemy inclines towards peace,
do thou also incline towards peace,
and trust God, for the Lord is the one that
heareth and knoweth all things.
And the servants of God,
Most gracious are those who walk on
the Earth in humility, and when we
address them, we say "Peace."

## NATIVE AMERICAN PRAYER FOR PEACE

Almighty God, the Great
Thumb we cannot evade to tie any knot;
the Roaring Thunder that splits mighty trees:
the all-seeing Lord up on high who sees
even the footprints of an antelope on
a rock mass here on Earth.
You are the one who does
not hesitate to respond to our call.
You are the cornerstone of peace.

## JEWISH PRAYER FOR PEACE

Come let us go up the mountain of the Lord,
that we may walk the paths of the Most High.
And we shall beat our swords into ploughshares,
and our spears into pruning hooks.
Nation shall not lift up sword against nation—
neither shall they learn war any more.
And none shall be afraid, for the mouth of the
Lord of Hosts has spoken.

"When I despair, I remember that all through history the ways of truth and love have always won. There have been tyrants and murderers, and for a time they can seem invincible, but in the end they always fall. Think of it—always."

Mahatma Gandhi

This prayer was first said in Persian by 'Abdu'l-Bahá on 5th May 1912 in Chicago, Illinois, during His tour of North America. 'Abdu'l-Bahá is the eldest son and appointed successor of Bahá'u'lláh, the Prophet Who founded the Bahá'í Faith. There is no special devotional language in the Bahá'í Faith and the prayers and scriptures of Bahá'u'lláh and 'Abdu'l-Bahá have been translated into hundreds of languages worldwide. Setswana is my mother-tongue and that of the Batswana people of Botswana and South Africa. The Batswana are renowned as a peace-loving people who avoid conflict and war. "War doesn't draw water out of the desert well," says a Setswana proverb, "rather it draws blood; it spares neither serf nor prince." The Sacred Writings of the Bahá'í Faith share a remarkable affinity with the democratic tradition of the Batswana in exalting consultation as the key to solving conflict: "Take ye counsel together in all matters," writes Bahá'u'lláh, "inasmuch as consultation is the lamp of guidance which leadeth the way, and is the bestower of understanding." For centuries it has been the tradition of my people to discuss problems in democratic village councils at which the chief acts more as chairman

than as ruler'. All citizens of Botswana, whatever their faith, were appalled by the inhumanity of the attack on America on the 11th of September, and there was an outpouring of sympathy for the innocent victims. As a Motswana I am proud that there has been no persecution of our Moslem brethren in my country, no displays of religious intolerance, no calls for revenge. As a Bahá'í, I take comfort in the words of Bahá'u'lláh, Who writes as follows: "Consort with the followers of all religions in a spirit of friendliness and fellowship. Blessed are such as hold fast to the cord of kindliness and tender mercy and are free from animosity and hatred. Of old it hath been revealed: 'Love of one's country is an element of the Faith of God.' The Tongue of Grandeur hath, however, in the day of His manifestation proclaimed: 'It is not his to boast who loveth his country, but it is his who loveth the world.'"

Lucretia Molalanyana 'Lally' Warren

# BAHÁ'Í PRAYER FOR PEACE

O Thou kind Lord! Thou hast created all humanity from the same stock. Thou hast decreed that all shall belong to the same household. In Thy Holy Presence they are all Thy servants, and all mankind are sheltered beneath Thy Tabernacle; all have gathered together at Thy Table of Bounty; all are illumined through the light of Thy Providence.

O God! Thou art kind to all, Thou hast provided for all, dost shelter all, conferrest life upon all. Thou hast endowed each and all with talents and faculties, and all are submerged in the Ocean of Thy Mercy.

O Thou kind Lord! Unite all. Let the religions agree and make the nations one, so that they may see each other as one family and the whole earth as one home. May they all live together in perfect harmony.

O God! Raise aloft the banner of the oneness of mankind.

O God! Establish the Most Great Peace. Cement Thou, O God, the hearts together.

O Thou kind Father, God! Gladden our hearts through the fragrance of Thy love. Brighten our eyes through the Light of Thy Guidance. Delight our ears with the melody of Thy Word, and shelter us all in the Stronghold of Thy Providence.

Thou art the Mighty and Powerful, Thou art the Forgiving and Thou art the One Who overlooketh the shortcomings of all mankind.

*'Abdu'l-Bahá*

"Amazing Grace" was composed by John Newton for services at Olney, in Buckinghamshire, England, where he served for many years as a curate. It was first published in 1779 in the collection "Olney Hymns," with the title "Faith's Review and Expectation." It is possibly the best-known hymn ever written. Newton is popularly considered to have written it one night after nearly being tossed overboard in a violent North Atlantic storm while working on a slave ship. Newton—who until that day had been known by his fellow sailors for his coarse reputation (he even earned the nickname "The Great Blasphemer")—the story goes, believed that his survival was through an act of God. Newton's mother had raised him to be a pious, educated man. She taught him to read the Scripture, hymns and poems by the age of three. She died just before Newton turned seven. At eleven, he took up his father's profession as a merchant seaman. During his many years at sea, Newton had rejected his mother's values, and even tried to break the faith of those around him. After his epiphany at sea, Newton changed his ways. At the age of thirty nine, John Newton became a preacher, a profession he would continue until his death forty three years later.

## AMAZING GRACE

Amazing grace! How sweet the sound
That saved a wretch like me!
I once was lost, but now am found;
Was blind, but now I see.

'Twas grace that taught my heart to fear,
And grace my fears relieved;
How precious did that grace appear
The hour I first believed.

Through many dangers, toils and snares,
I have already come;
'Tis grace hath brought me safe thus far,
And grace will lead me home.

The Lord has promised good to me,
His Word my hope secures;
He will my Shield and Portion be,
As long as life endures.

Yea, when this flesh and heart shall fail,
And mortal life shall cease,
I shall possess, within the veil,
A life of joy and peace.

The earth shall soon dissolve like snow,
The sun forbear to shine;
But God, Who called me here below,
Shall be forever mine.

When we've been there ten thousand years,
Bright shining as the sun,
We've no less days to sing God's praise
Than when we'd first begun.

John Newton

# ADVENT PEACE PRAYER

Lord, we know what peace is. Peace is a mother tenderly holding her child. Peace is a firm handshake of trust between friends. Peace is complete emotional security. Peace is living unencumbered with a full sense of joy. Peace is expressing Thanksgiving for concrete blessings.

For the peace gained from the love and memory
of spouses and children, we thank You…
For the peace gained from the love and memory
of parents and grandparents, we thank You…
For the peace gained from the kindness and support
of friends, we thank You…
For the peace gained when the music of God is sung,
we thank You…

Peace is elusive. There are raging storms in every life. Tragedy, grief and pain will visit everyone. Yet, each person's life is graced by moments and periods of real happiness. For these presents of peace and joy, past, present and future, we offer our deepest gratitude.

Help us to understand that peace must be waged. We must resist the gun, the bomb, "realistic politics," unkind words, personal betrayals, anger, depression, despair and rage. Give us the strength to overcome these demons. Help us maintain personal power within ourselves, so we can pass this liberating power to others.

Give hope and courage to all who struggle with debilitating illness, grief and loneliness. Help them to understand: All chains will be broken.

John Devries

## ISLAMIC PRAYER FOR PEACE

We think of Thee, worship Thee, bow to Thee as the Creator of this Universe; we seek refuge in Thee, the Truth, our only support. Thou art the Ruler, the barge in this ocean of endless births and deaths.

In the name of Allah, the beneficent, the merciful. Praise be to the Lord of the Universe who has created us and made us into tribes and nations. Give us wisdom that we may know each other and not despise all things. We shall abide by thy Peace. And, we shall remember the servants of God are those who walk on this earth in humility and, when we address them, we shall say Peace unto us all.

## JEWISH PRAYER FOR PEACE

May the blessing of peace unfold and infuse,
embrace and intertwine
all of Israel and all the world.

Eternal wellspring of peace—
May we be drenched with the longing for peace
that we may give ourselves over to peace
until the earth overflows with peace
as living waters overflow the seas.

May the blessing of peace unfold and infuse,
embrace and intertwine
all of Israel and all the world.

As we bless the source of life
So we are blessed.

# INDEX

Editor's note: In the making of Prayers for Peace, we tried to include prayers that represent the widest number of faiths possible. It was nearly impossible, however, to represent all of them. Here is a list of just a few religions, each of which is striving to reach the same understanding of mankind's place in the world:

| | | | |
|---|---|---|---|
| African Traditional & Diasporic | Fijian Religion | Church | Society of Friends (Quakers) |
| Agama Tirtha | Fon Religion | Nuer | Spiritism |
| Ahmadiyya | Gabars | Orthodox Church | Sthanakavasis |
| Akan | Ganda Religion | Parsis | Sufism |
| Aleut/Inuit Religion | Greek Orthodox | Pentecostalism | Sunni |
| Amish | Guarni-Kaiowa | PL Kyodan | Svetambara |
| Anglican | Hare Krishna Movement | Presbyterianism | Taoism |
| Australian Aborigine Religion | Hinduism | Protestantism | Tenrikyo |
| Baha'i Faith | Islam | Pueblo | Tensho Kotai Jingukyo |
| Bantu Baptists | Jainism | Rastafarianism | Theravada |
| Batak Religion | Jehovah's Witness | Reconstructionist | Unification Church |
| Buddhism | Jesuits | Roman Catholic | Unitarian-Universalism |
| Cao Dai | Juche | Sakya Tradition | Vaishnavites |
| Chinese Traditional Religion | Judiasim | Scientology | Veerashaivas |
| Christianity | Lamaism | Seicho-No-Ie | Wahhabiyah Movement |
| Confucianism | Latter-Day Saints | Sekai Kyuseikyo | Yoruba |
| Congregationalism | Liberal Protestant | Seventh-Day Adventists | Zen Buddhism |
| Digambaras | Lutheranism | Shaivites | Zenrinkai |
| Druze | Mahayana | Shi'ite | Zorostrainism |
| Ennokyo | Methodism | Shilluk Religion | |
| | Mormons | Shinto | |
| | Native American | Sikhism | |

Editor's note: In the making of Prayers for Peace, we tried to include prayers that represent the widest number of faiths possible. It was nearly impossible, however, to represent all of them. Here is a list of just a few religions, each of which is striving to reach the same understanding of mankind's place in the world:

| | | | |
|---|---|---|---|
| African Traditional & Diasporic | Fijian Religion | Church | Society of Friends (Quakers) |
| Agama Tirtha | Fon Religion | Nuer | Spiritism |
| Ahmadiyya | Gabars | Orthodox Church | Sthanakavasis |
| Akan | Ganda Religion | Parsis | Sufism |
| Aleut/Inuit Religion | Greek Orthodox | Pentecostalism | Sunni |
| Amish | Guarni-Kaiowa | PL Kyodan | Svetambara |
| Anglican | Hare Krishna | Presbyterianism | Taoism |
| Australian Aborigine Religion | Movement | Protestantism | Tenrikyo |
| | Hinduism | Pueblo | Tensho Kotai |
| Baha'i Faith | Islam | Rastafarianism | Jingukyo |
| Bantu Baptists | Jainism | Reconstructionist | Theravada |
| Batak Religion | Jehovah's Witness | Roman Catholic | Unification Church |
| Buddhism | Jesuits | Sakya Tradition | Unitarian-Universalism |
| Cao Dai | Juche | Scientology | |
| Chinese Traditional Religion | Judiasim | Seicho-No-Ie | Vaishnavites |
| | Lamaism | Sekai Kyuseikyo | Veerashaivas |
| Christianity | Latter-Day Saints | Seventh-Day Adventists | Wahhabiyah Movement |
| Confucianism | Liberal Protestant | Shaivites | |
| Congregationalism | Lutheranism | Shi'ite | Yoruba |
| Digambaras | Mahayana | Shilluk Religion | Zen Buddhism |
| Druze | Methodism | Shinto | Zenrinkai |
| Ennokyo | Mormons | Sikhism | Zorostrainism |
| | Native American | | |

THIS BOOK IS A GIFT FROM

_____

PRESENTED TO

_____

ON THIS DAY

_____